No Pain, No Gain

HOPE FOR THOSE WHO STRUGGLE

JOHN R. WIMMER

A Ballantine/Epiphany Book
BALLANTINE BOOKS • NEW YORK

A Ballantine/Epiphany Book

Grateful acknowledgment is made to the following for permission to reprint previously published material:

Avon Books: lyrics from *The Fantastics* by Tom Jones and Harvey Schmidt. Copyright © 1964, published by Drama Book Specialists/Publishers, New York, 1968. Used with permission.

Mary Ann Bernard: excerpts from the poem "Resurrection" by Mary Ann Bernard. Taken from *A Guide to Prayer for Ministers and Other Servants* by Rueben P. Job and Norman Shawchuck. Copyright © 1983 by Upper Room, Nashville TN. Used by permission of the author.

Alfred A. Knopf, Inc.: Excerpts from "On Pain" by Kahlil Gibran. Reprinted from *The Prophet*, by Kahlil Gibran by permission of Alfred A. Knopf, Inc. Copyright 1923 by Kahlil Gibran and renewed 1951 by Administrators C.T.A. of Kahlil Gibran Estate, and Mary G. Gibran.

National Council of Churches: Excerpts from the Revised Standard Version of the Oxford Annotated Bible. Published by Oxford University Press. Copyright 1946, 1952, © 1971, 1973. Used by permission.

Library of Congress Cataloging in Publication Data

Wimmer, John R., 1956–
    No pain, no gain.

    Includes bibliographical references.
    1. Christian life—Methodist authors. 2. Suffering—
Religious aspects—Christianity. 3. Theodicy. I. Title.
BV4501.2.W564   1985   248.4'87606   84–24241
ISBN 0-345-32181-2

Manufactured in the United States of America
Text design by Holly Johnson

First Edition: November 1985

10 9 8 7 6 5 4 3 2 1

For, and with, Jan

There is a curious paradox
That no one can explain.
Who understands the secret
Of the reaping of the grain?

Who understands why Spring is born
Out of Winter's laboring pain?
Or why we all must die a bit
Before we grow again.

—*The Fantasticks*

CONTENTS

Introduction   xiii

I.   Pain   1

Our "Painless" Society   3
Embracing Pain   6
Alone with Pain   9
Pain and the Cross   11
"A Curious Paradox"   14

II.   Gain   17

Discipline and Learning   19
Refining Faith   22
Mature Faith   24
Finding Meaning in Our Trials   26
Everything Works Together   29
Beginnings of Hope   33

III.   Hope   37

       Hope and the Human Spirit   39
       Grief and Hope   42
       The Road Less Traveled: God's Hope
           Displayed   44
       The Hope of God's People   47
       Endless Hope?   51

IV.   Help   55

       Helpful Prayer   57
       Helpful People   61
       Help and Healing   63
       The Wounded Healer   66
       Mance   69

       Postscript   75

ACKNOWLEDGMENTS

This is the most difficult page of this book to write, for there are many more persons who deserve thanks than can be mentioned here. To all these people whose support is so valued, I can only hope to express gratitude in other significant ways. Among these there are a few whom I especially wish to acknowledge.

First I want to thank my spouse, Jan Blaising, for her insights, her creativity, and her integrity, which have influenced this book beyond what words can adequately express. In fact, we have spent so many hours together sharing and talking about these matters that the difference between her thoughts and mine expressed here are virtually indistinguishable. The hours we share together make me more thankful each day she is the one with whom I share life.

Our families, Wimmers and Blaisings, deserve thanks for their seemingly endless patience and loving support that has meant so much for many years.

Also I express my gratitude to Adolf Hansen (whose unique ability to combine spirituality and scholarship has influenced me greatly), Rob Rollins, John VanVactor, Jack Pavy, Brian Witwer, and the Wednesday A.M. Study Group at First United Methodist Church in West Lafayette, Indiana, for their ideas, friendship, and caring. Special appreciation also belongs to Michelle Rapkin of Ballantine Books for her wise and gracious editorial guidance, as well as to Marjorie Braman and Toni Simmons.

INTRODUCTION

*P*erhaps no one really knows who coined the phrase "no pain, no gain," although it sounds like something the ever-winning Green Bay Packers coach Vince Lombardi would have said.

The idea is not only basic vocabulary for striving athletes but can be employed by struggling Christians as well.

I vividly recall the first time I heard the words. Having faced the fact that I needed to lose weight, I'd begun a regimen of dieting and daily jogging. So proud was I of my progress that one evening I decided to show off my achievement: I invited a friend to run with me. I didn't know he was in much better physical condition than I. By the time we had run two-and-a-half miles (already half a mile more than I usually ran by myself), discomfort overcame pride and I begged my friend to stop our running. I gasped out the news that my lungs ached and my legs felt as if they would soon fall off! "Come on, John!" came the response. "*No pain, no gain!*"

Wise coaches place that maxim on bulletin boards and posters in weight-workout rooms and athletic locker rooms; they know their would-be disciples need encouraging reminders that athletic excellence has a price tag.

"No pain, no gain" implies that in order for you to be a good athlete, for you to become a true champion, you must be willing to persevere through the pain. Your efforts will cost you; you must extend yourself to the very edge of your endurance—to the point where you experience pain. Yet beyond that threshold lie greater endurance, confidence, and ability than if this pain and gain is not encountered.

As my friend urged me on that evening while we ran, I certainly felt intense pain. Yet his words reminded me of the progress I'd already made in both dieting and distance running. At first I had lost very little weight and was capable of running only half a mile. But soon, and with no great difficulty, I could run three-fourths of a mile and then a mile. Through my steady exercise and substantial reductions in caloric intake, pounds gradually but consistently melted away. As my mind wandered on these thoughts, and I continued forcing one foot in front of the other, somehow my physical pain seemed a little less intense. And with the first stirrings of faith in those encouraging words "no pain, no gain," I was able to summon the courage to run still farther. That night I experienced the thrill of running past the three-mile marker for the first time.

Then I collapsed!

Nevertheless, even as I was catching my breath and rubbing my sore legs, I knew pleasure, even joy I would not have known had I quit earlier.

I've learned a couple of things since that day I jogged with my friend. One of them is that if I quit jogging, I'd gain thirty pounds—no pain, plenty of gained weight! I also reflected that "no pain, no gain" is not only an athletic principle. Skilled musicians, physicians, business persons, academicians, artists—people in these and other walks of life know that the pain resulting from the struggle of study and practice grows into greater levels of proficiency, healing, and growth. We discover deeper-lying planes of unexplored territory outside us and unrealized creativity within.

Yet, I believe that "no pain, no gain" expresses an even more profound *spiritual* principle. It is one of the basic laws of the universe God is creating; it is a central reality of the Christian faith, in which we suffer, learn, grow, and rejoice. For just like the athlete, a Christian grows in spiritual strength and stamina from having experienced and worked through painful struggles.

That's the opposite of what we are sometimes told Christians ought to be like. We may wrongly assume that as Christians, we should not have any problems—and if we do, it is because we lack faith. Worse still, when we experience spiritual and emotional struggle, too often we are made to feel that we are being punished by God for some sin or wrongful deed we have committed or some good deed neglected. Because we hurt and believe God may be responsible, we naturally feel like angrily shouting at God, "Why are you doing this to me?!" Immediately we are filled with remorse for worsening our unknown sin by shouting at the Creator! We then have no choice but to give up the hope that God will help; to ponder the mystery of our eternal fate as we seethe with pain, loneliness, and anger.

Why do we feel pain in our struggles? Why must we continue to deal with those people and situations that produce suffering? Where is God when we feel this pain?

Questions directed toward God about the nature of life are as old as the stories we read in the accounts of the wandering Israelites questioning God's care as they searched for the Promised Land (Numbers 13–14) or the exiled people bewailing God's absence as they felt the pain of separation from Jerusalem's Temple during their captivity in Babylon (Jeremiah and Lamentations). And there are no easy answers to such searching questions. In the New Testament, probably the most significant question ever asked, the one still echoing through the heavens into our hearts, was uttered by Jesus himself, when he cried from the pain and agony of the cross, "My God, my God, why hast thou forsaken me?" (Matt. 27:46).

As these passages from the Bible show us, in the midst of the pain and suffering we experience in our lives, we must not only cope with the pain itself, but also wrestle with the burden of trying to understand why we must face such painful trials to begin with.

We will not attempt here to answer the rhetorical question of why suffering and evil exist in the world (although we will acknowledge and discuss it). Rather, we will try to understand as best we can what progress is being made by applying the "no pain, no gain" principle in our spiritual life as we engage in struggles. We cannot always understand or control many of the things that happen to us, but we can play a major role in determining our *response* to the struggles we experience. So it is to this response that we will turn most of our attention.

That focus may or may not help banish the pain we face; yet we may begin to understand more fully that every struggle confronting us is an opportunity for spiritual growth. If we make the decision to seize this opportunity for growth, we will indeed experience newer, deeper, more meaningful dimensions of the life God graciously gives us in abundance.

Therefore, to those running "the race that is set before us" (Heb. 12:1) whose lungs ache and whose legs feel as if they will soon fall off—let us discover that gain will come from our pain!

Part I: PAIN

They have an inadequate view of suffering.
—Helmut Thielicke describing the
greatest defect among
American Christians

Our "Painless" Society

Pain hurts!

It seems silly to say something so obvious. Yet this simple statement is one of the hardest lessons we must learn in life. Because we have "an inadequate view of suffering," we act as if pain does not hurt. Many of us try desperately, some of us all of our lives, to deny that pain is a fact of life.

I was both amused and saddened by a story recently told to me by my sister and her husband just before they were blessed with the birth of their first child, Ryan. Like most other couples having children, they were in the process of deciding which method of labor assistance they would use at the time of birth. In enumerating the benefits and shortcomings she had experienced in using one particular method, a friend of my sister's warned her, "There's one major flaw in that program: No one told me that having the baby was going to *hurt!*"

Seldom do people tell us that certain aspects of living are going to be painful. Growing into adulthood—a process that never ceases—presents struggles common to us all but experienced differently by each of us. As some feel the joyous pain of childbirth, others nurse the hurt of infertility. Youthful friendships and peer pressures, dating and breaking up, schoolwork and vocational decisions all have certain growing pains associated with them. Yet adulthood brings its own trying "passages" involving occupational stresses, or unemployment, marriage/family issues, the loss of loved ones, serious illness, midlife crises, aging parents, accidents, retirement, and a host of other stresses provoked by everyday living!

In the face of this reality, our culture tries in countless ways to inform us as we mature from childhood into adulthood that life ought to remain a painless activity. From the time we are infants, it seems, we are soothed and shielded from the discomforts of life. We are pampered with cottony soft diapers, baby powder, and extra-gentle shampoo. Loving us, our parents attempt to smile away the little hurts we encounter. We are cuddled when we cry, fed when hungry, and sometimes spoiled with attention by relatives and friends who love cute little babies.

Love and attention are great! Embracing love and gentle care shown to us as infants and toddlers instills within us an invaluable gift: the message that we are loved and lovable. Yet even with the best love and care (and the most ambitious attempts at spoiling us by proud parents and gift-bearing grandparents), we cannot help but occasionally develop a painful diaper rash! More painfully, some of us, as children, don't receive the care we need and deserve.

As we grow older, we may spend much time and money protecting ourselves from hurt, just as others sheltered us as children. We rely on aspirin to relieve our stress-induced headaches, relaxants to ease overworked muscles, antacids to soothe overworked stomachs. Yet is the upset stomach our real problem or a symptom of a deeper malaise?

Consciously or unconsciously, we experience some pain almost daily resulting from interactions with other people. At work, home, or school, our days include an emotional mixture of such ingredients as frustration, pressure, and competition. And beyond day-to-day discomforts are the more severe physical and emotional disturbances we inevitably face. Tragedies may precipitate deeply trying times, forcing upon us unpleasant facts of life we would rather avoid. A changing economy and cultural expectations may place new pressures on marriages, engagements, parent-child relations, vocational plans. The struggle resulting from such stress may often produce painful decisions that may result in marital or family separations, divorce, career changes, moving, or some other action entailing personal sacrifices. Ours is *not* a painless society!

Wrestling with difficult decisions, we find that living hurts, and we are tempted to seek ways to escape our struggle. In extreme cases we may try to dull the ache through the use and abuse of alcohol or drugs. After all, anyone who has ever sat in front of a TV set knows that quickly ridding ourselves of discomfort is simple and, of course, always desirable: We have only to buy the more powerful antacid, the painkiller that gets into the blood faster to fight our headache, the hemorrhoid ointment that will let us sit more comfortably in our easy chair. Advertisers pay out huge sums in promoting the idea that for a small price we can live in a painless environment.

In such a climate, if we find that our marriage involves more struggle than we had anticipated, divorce or separation can seem to be an easy solution to the immediate pain. In other cases, avoiding difficult marital or other family problems may be a method of evading or postponing terrible hurts. Even if we avoid these more extreme reactions to pain, we may construct imaginary walls around our inner emotional selves, thinking we can be insulated from truly feeling pain.

Some persons even look to the church, or religion, as a monastery to which they can flee the discomfort of the "real world" by cloaking themselves within seemingly religious responses to pain. Yet this use of an escapist "faith" is no better than others' use of alcohol or drugs.

Sometimes an escape into church is valid; it may provide a place where we can, temporarily, leave the trials of daily living behind; where we may find an answer to a specific problem; or where we may find closer communication with

God. This differs greatly from the extremist reaction of "escaping" permanently into the church in order to hide from "real life." Faith should not be used as a method of escape!

After the fleeting numbness has faded from these attempted escapes, we learn that the struggles and sore spots have never really gone away; and in company with this realization, our struggles revisit us at an even more oppressive level of intensity.

Embracing Pain

Given our "inadequate view of suffering," it is no wonder we find it difficult to face our struggles. Yet before we are able to experience the relief, gain, and growth from the pain struggle produces, we must first come face-to-face with the fact that if we want to feel the gain we must first feel the pain.

But it's important to remember that there are two kinds of sufferers. Some people—athletes, for example—willingly take on pain for the specific purpose of self-improvement. Others do not ask for pain yet must experience it no matter how unwillingly.

Ralph Sockman, in his book *The Meaning of Suffering*, points out that some types of pain are perceived as pleasurable. Of course, one's tolerance for self-chosen pain must be very high. Sockman tells of an encounter with a football coach who stated that one of the prime qualifications for a top-notch player is that "he must *enjoy* pain."

We can afford to "enjoy" pain when we voluntarily assume the pain of physical conditioning for the pleasure of sport; or when we choose to take on the emotional struggle of therapy for the pleasure of personal growth; or when we accept the sacrifices of dieting in order to enjoy losing weight! When one chooses pain, the person may realize from the very beginning certain sacrifices must be made in order for the desired gains in strength or growth to be achieved.

But what about the pain we do not inflict upon ourselves? Are those who do not choose their pain supposed to enjoy it as the coach said a good player should?

There are—and should be—definite differences in attitude and motivation between those who willingly encounter pain and those who are forced to deal with intense pain due to mistakes, accidents, illnesses, death, or the not-so-mere everyday tasks that pile up and leave us feeling victimized by life. Although we rarely want to, if we are to enjoy the benefit of gains in our emotional/spiritual life, *we must face our struggle and embrace our pain!* Or as W. C. Fields put it: "There comes a time in the affairs of humanity when you must take the bull by the tail and face the situation!"

At the prospect of thoroughly unpleasant situations, we may think it easier to deal with our problems by simply ignoring them—maybe they'll go away. As we have seen, we may also try to elude the problem by numbing the hurt. The truth is that such avoidance is like sweeping dirt under the carpet: Barring great good luck or a miracle, the problem is still there; it's only temporarily out of sight. And in choosing *not* to deal with pain, we usually find that not only does the hurt fail to go away, it also transfers itself into other areas of our lives.

When I first met Clifford, an elderly man I once knew, I did not like his sour personality; he seemed to lash out at nearly everyone he met. He was grumpy and short-tempered; he complained constantly—and he bitterly described as "stupid" nearly everything anyone did in his presence. I found out later from others who knew him well that he had not been that way before "the accident." A few years before, Clifford's only daughter had been killed in a car crash due to her own negligence in failing to take certain precautionary measures.

I remember the day Clifford first told me about his daughter's death. He began telling the story calmly, but became progressively more angry, finally reaching a climax of rage. He thrust his face at mine, shouting at me how "stupid" it was of his daughter to be so unconcerned with her own safety.

I recognized that tone of voice: The "stupid" sounded exactly like the "stupid" he so habitually applied to others in his dealings with them. When I commented that he seemed angry about his daughter's accident (hoping this would help Clifford draw out his anger), he quickly "got hold of himself" and almost immediately returned to a fake calmness. It seemed as if nothing had happened as he concluded tersely, "I'm not angry. It doesn't matter. It's over now."

But it *wasn't* over, and it *did* matter; he was angry and hurt and had not embraced those feelings in order to express them fully and honestly and let the healing begin. How tragic it was that to the end of his life he displayed the effects of deep pain while refusing to admit to harboring any feelings at all! Consequently, when I met Clifford five years after the tragic death of his daughter, this man who so desperately needed the love and care of other people to help heal his deep pain was repelling all who would offer their concern because his own inability to embrace his pain produced a very unattractive anger at others.

The primary key to embracing pain is to be *honest* about what is hurting us. But it is not always easy to identify the sources of our pain. Of course, when we experience such tragedy as the death of a loved one, most of us find it all too easy to determine the source of our grief; yet sometimes our hurts are disguised by very deeply ingrained avoidance techniques we have acquired or cultivated over years. Maybe we are too lazy or too scared to do the very demanding work of embracing pain—for contrary to what some believe, dealing with emotions is *very* hard work!—or it could be that we are afraid of other hurts we might lay bare if we honestly confront the sources of our distress. For often, when we are honest with our feelings, we find that accompanying our pain are clusters of other strong feelings that may include differing combinations of anger, guilt, rage, sadness, insecurity, disappointment, loneliness, confusion...the list is long. When we are rigorously honest, we may suddenly find ourselves struggling with many more open questions than we anticipated. We may feel bogged down in analyzing and working through these many-faceted clusters of feelings. *Yet we must embrace these feelings no matter how painful.*

When we realize the extreme demands of embracing pain, we can find the courage to face them by remembering our ultimate goal: determining our best response to our hurts and learning the lessons taught us through our struggles (as we shall see later).

Alone with Pain

It is during the earliest stages of our honest recognition of our pain (in which we may identify other feeling clusters and the sources of our pain) that we may feel the most alone, hurt, misunderstood, and tempted with giving up. It seems that no one really cares or understands. Sometimes even God seems distant!

At stressful times like these it is helpful to know that other persons who have possessed great faith have felt this same way. Several of the Psalms give us insight into what it feels like to be in this lonely and bitter place where we embrace and wrestle with pain. In fact, an entire group of Psalms, called the "laments," reveals the struggles of the psalmists in understanding their own suffering as they too asked, "Where are you, God?" Just a few of their words, ones resonating with our feelings:

> How long, O Lord? Wilt thou
> forget me for ever?
> How long wilt thou hide thy
> face from me?
> How long must I bear pain in my soul,
> and have sorrow in my heart all the day?
> Psalm 13:1–2

My wounds grow foul and fester
    because of my foolishness,
I am utterly bowed down and prostrate;
    all the day I go about mourning.

I am utterly spent and crushed;
    I groan because of the tumult of my heart.

Psalm 38:5–6, 8

I say to God, my rock:
    "Why hast thou forgotten me?
Why go I mourning
    because of the oppression of the enemy?"
As with a deadly wound in my body,
    my adversaries taunt me,
While they say to me continually,
    "Where is your God?"

Psalm 42:9–10

Although there are many times when the words of the Bible offer us inspiration and comfort, at other times they will not immediately soothe our feelings of loneliness in suffering.

In our own time, this reality has been expressed by William Sloane Coffin, pastor of Riverside Church in New York, when he lost his twenty-four-year-old son, Alex, in a tragic automobile accident. In an amazing gesture of courage and openness, not even two weeks after Alex's death, Coffin preached a sermon in which he shared part of his own grieving process with his congregation. Among the flood of sympathy letters he received were many from fellow ministers who, Coffin said, often "proved they knew their Bibles better than the human condition." He found little comfort, he said, from those who sought to give help by proclaiming that it was "God's will" for Alex to die. Coffin continued:

> The point is this: while the words of the Bible are true, grief renders them unreal. The reality of grief is the absence of God—"My God, my God, why hast

thou forsaken me?" The reality of grief is the solitude of pain, the feeling that your heart's in pieces, your mind's a blank, that "there is no joy the world can give like that it takes away" (Lord Byron).

The most painful reality of our struggles is the knowledge that no one else (including God) can suffer our pain for us. We feel alone in our pain.

Pain and the Cross

No matter who you are or no matter how much faith you may have (or not have), when you face and embrace your pain you will sometimes echo the psalmists and the Reverend William Sloane Coffin: "Where are you, God?" When we find God and our faith meaningful in our lives, it is perfectly natural, even wonderful that we ask such a question of God—no matter how agonizing it feels to utter the question! It is rather commonly thought that questioning is contrary to faith. Yet honest questioning may well be one of the most positive expressions of deep faithfulness. Doubt and searching questions can only exist where there is a deep level of love and respect—and God loves us and respects us enough to allow our doubts and questions!

The greatest comfort available to us all in our seemingly lonely, desertlike places of pain is remembering that Jesus himself felt the excruciating pain of the cross. (In fact, the word "excruciating" comes from the Latin for "to crucify.") For in his own moment of agony, Jesus, too, cried out the words from Psalm 22, "My God, my God, why hast thou forsaken me?" (Matt. 27:46).

From the cross of Christ and these words he spoke there, we can learn much about God's presence amid the suffering of the world and in our own suffering. For nothing shows us more clearly that suffering and pain are a part of life to be embraced than the way Jesus faced the sorrow he knew was inevitable if he stayed on the path to Jerusalem. He too was tempted with avoiding or escaping the struggle ("Father, if it be possible, let this cup pass from me." [Matt. 26:39]). Who among us has been more painfully honest with God about our feelings? And certainly Jesus did not *want* to suffer the pain he was to embrace. But he went on to say, "not as I will, but as thou wilt." Of course, Jesus suffered an agonizing, humiliating death—seemingly, the most useless pain anyone can suffer!

Yet not only do we learn from the crucifixion that Jesus was tempted with avoiding pain and questioning God's presence; the cross points us toward another very important realization when we consider the question, "Where is God when we suffer?" For through the witness of the life and death of Christ, God sent us a message that God did not spare even Jesus the pain of life and death. Nor, since God *was* Christ, did God spare himself agony. Even when his enormous suffering on a lonely cross overcame Jesus and he gave way to doubt—"My God, my God, why hast thou forsaken me?"— we see by this very act that God was there in the suffering, showing us what God is like. *God shows us in the cross that God is also one who suffers—one who is willing to suffer with us as well as for us!* This does not take away *our* suffering; it shows us that even in our darkest despair, God is there with us. Although God will not take away our suffering, God helps us work through the pain by giving us strength, comfort, hope, and courage. Bishop Mack Stokes said it well:

> Calvary was not new to God. It expressed the heart of God. As soon as there were men [and women] that sinned, hearts that broke, souls that despaired, God's great heart knew the cross that was from the beginning himself. This has been beautifully expressed in the book of Revelation where we read of the Lamb slain from the foundation of the world (Rev. 13:8). So the crucifixion is ever present in the heart of God. And the crucifixion is daily reenacted whenever sin

and sadness flourish. And this too fills us with Godly
sorrow and pulls us mightily into the marvelous fel-
lowship with God.

(*Major United Methodist Beliefs*, p. 67)

The popular mystic Kahlil Gibran captured the connec-
tion between the no pain, no gain principle and the idea of
God as a fellow sufferer in his words on "Pain" in *The Prophet*:

> And a woman spoke, saying, Tell us of Pain.
> And he said:
> Your pain is the breaking of the shell that encloses
>   your understanding.
> Even as the stone of the fruit must break, that its
>   heart may stand in the sun, so must you know
>   pain.
>
> And could you keep your heart in wonder at the
>   daily miracles of your life, your pain would
>   not seem less wondrous than your joy;
> And you would accept the seasons of your heart,
>   even as you have always accepted the seasons
>   that pass over your fields.
> And you would watch with serenity through the
>   winters of your grief.
>
> Much of your pain is self-chosen.
> It is the bitter potion by which the physician
>   within you heals your sick self.
> Therefore trust the physician, and drink his remedy
>   in silence and tranquility:
> For his hand, though heavy and hard, is guided by
>   the tender hand of the Unseen,
> And the cup he brings, though it burn your lips,
>   has been fashioned of the clay which the Potter
>   has moistened with His own sacred tears.

"A Curious Paradox"

*W*hen we realize that God has shown us in Christ that God suffers along with us, our pleas to God that we be spared from struggle and pain are understandable in their honesty; yet to expect God to shelter us from suffering is to miss the meaning of suffering taught us by the cross.

One of the paradoxes of life is that we sometimes must hurt before we can grow. Looking a little more closely, we learn that by this same paradox we see the meaning of life through death, joy through sorrow, hope through despair, and love through hate. It is through pain that we see growth, through the cross that we see God.

At the beginning of this book are printed the poignant words spoken at the close of the musical *The Fantasticks*:

> There is a curious paradox
> That no one can explain.
> Who understands the secret
> Of the reaping of the grain?
>
> Who understands why Spring is born
> Out of Winter's laboring pain?
> Or why we all must die a bit
> Before we grow again.

There is a sense in which we will never understand or fully explain why our lives must in part be painful. No matter how earnest our prayers, no matter how penetrating or intelligent our questioning, we will not ever thoroughly know *why*.

But we do know that in the spring the delicate shoots of beautifully budding flowers break the soil left hard and barren from the winter's bitter cold. We know that one tiny planted seed, if nurtured to maturity, yields much more grain than the one originally sacrificed to the ground. We know that a pruned fruit tree will bear more and larger fruit than one left unattended. And we know that our scrapes and cuts and bruises, as well as most of our minor and major surgeries, eventually are made well through the miraculous process we call healing.

The point: That there is manifest in our world a process of hurt and healing, practice and proficiency, pain and gain suggests that this is the process by which God works spiritual growth in our lives. Although God may be responsible, ultimately, in allowing this painful process to enter creation, God remains present throughout this painful process, faithfully nurturing and comforting and giving growth to all of us who live, hurt, struggle, and learn. In our lives, as in the world about us, there must be rain and sunshine, night and day, winter and spring!

Further, to deny pain is to fail to listen to very important communication from God. For pain is the sign given to us telling us we are in danger and must make a response to work our way through the danger by seeking help. When in pain, we know something is wrong that needs to change! Pain is part of—even essential to—the miracle of healing. For our discomfort is an excellent motivation for us to seek help from God, our church, our families and friends, medical and psychological professionals, books, or whatever else may be able to assist us in working through our hurt.

While we struggle, however, pain is not all we feel. God has tossed out a lifeline for us to hold on to: *hope*, which can sustain us and help us pull ourselves toward the shores of progress. And with hope, we also have faith; faith not that we will be spared pain but that God will lead us *through* the pain and struggle to our goal of growth. Therefore, in our struggle to understand God's will, let us not concentrate solely on our pain (although we know we are to accept it). Let us look with hope and faith toward attaining new, richer experience of the precious life God has given us.

Part II: GAIN

For everything there is a season, and a time for every matter under heaven:

 a time to be born, and a time to die;

 . . . .

 a time to break down, and a time to build up;
 a time to weep, and a time to laugh;
 a time to mourn, and a time to dance;

 . . . .

 a time to embrace, and a time to refrain from
  embracing.

 . . . .

What gain has the worker from his toil?
      (Ecclesiastes 3:1,2a,3b,4,5b,9)

Discipline and Learning

We have seen that asking God, "Why am I suffering?" is a healthy response to pain, one appropriate to a person who considers God very important; but that seeking God's deliverance from struggle may not be fruitful. Allowing unrelenting questioning to plague one's heart diverts attention and energy from where they need to be placed: on becoming whole.

In embracing our pain we must guard against allowing it to get the best of us — which may happen if we concentrate on what seems to us to be the futility of our struggle. It is crucial for us to realize that when we do this we are allowing our pain to control us: As Leo Buscaglia has written, "When we cling to pain we end up punishing ourselves." Rather, we should learn to manage our pain so that we may move ourselves out of the danger of which our pain warns us.

So instead of intensifying the hurt by calling undue amounts of attention to it, we must work toward focusing our attention on our response to pain — and begin to realize the growth that will result from our efforts.

Having summarized the faith of great persons from the

Old Testament, the writer of Hebrews, using athletic imagery, admonishes us to concentrate on a faithful response to suffering rather than "cling" to it:

> Therefore, since we are surrounded by so great a cloud of witnesses, let us lay aside every weight, and sin which clings so closely, and let us run with perseverance the race that is set before us, looking to Jesus the pioneer and perfecter of our faith, who for the joy that was set before him endured the cross, despising the shame, and is seated at the right hand of the throne of God.
>
> Consider him who endured from sinners such hostility against himself, so that you may not grow weary or fainthearted. In your struggle against sin you have not resisted to the point of shedding your blood. And have you forgotten the exhortation which addresses you as sons?—
>
> "My son, do not regard lightly the
> discipline of the Lord,
> nor lose courage when you are punished
> by him.
> For the Lord disciplines him who he loves,
> and chastises every son whom he
> receives."
>
> It is for discipline that you have to endure. God is treating you as sons; for what son is there whom a father does not discipline? If you are left without discipline, in which all have participated, then you are illegitimate children and not sons. Besides this, we have had earthly fathers to discipline us and we respected them. Shall we not much more be subject to the Father of spirits and live? For they disciplined us for a short time at their pleasure, but he disciplines us for our own good, that we may share his holiness.

And then the most important part:

> For the moment all discipline seems painful rather

than pleasant; later it yields the peaceful fruit of righteousness to those who have been trained by it.

(Heb. 12:1-11)

The image of the heavenly parent used in this passage may evoke a recollection of the earthly parent who dragged us by the ear out behind the woodshed to warm our seat! Who has not heard a loving parent utter, at just such a "bottom-warming" occasion, "This is going to hurt me more than it hurts you!" Few of those on the literal receiving end believe this parental cliché. Yet strangely, when we become parents who must at times punish our own children, these words about discipline suddenly speak truth.

The original Greek word translated as "discipline" in the scripture passage offered above is derived from the same root word as "to instruct" and "to learn." Therefore, the "discipline" of that passage is not necessarily to be associated exclusively with punishment (although certainly the element of punishment is also present in the passage). Actually, this periscope emphasizes discipline as a learning, growing, deepening experience. In other words, this passage tells us that when we are in the midst of suffering, we should view the "discipline" we find there as an opportunity for spiritual growth rather than as punishment from an angry, capricious parent figure. Although this discipline is painful, later we find that our suffering yields the peaceful righteousness that comes from God.

In his fine book *Where Is God When It Hurts?* Philip Yancey points out that the New Testament describes at least five ways in which suffering can yield spiritual growth. In essence, Yancey says that the role of suffering in our faith is that it "turns us to God" when we might otherwise not have been willing to seek and receive God's help. For suffering, the Bible says, can:

1. Refine our faith   (1 Pet. 1:5-7)
2. Produce maturity of faith   (James 1:2-4)
3. Allow us an opportunity to display God's works
                                                 (John 9:10-13)

4. Conform us more nearly to Christ's image
(Rom. 8:28,29)
5. Produce in us Christian perseverance and character
(Rom. 5:3–8)

Let us take a closer look into these areas of spiritual growth.

Refining Faith

*I*n common with the book of Revelation, 1 Peter is a letter written when persecution of the early Christians by the Roman State was rampant. Citizenship in the Roman Empire demanded full allegiance, and Christian loyalty, it was thought, undermined imperial rule. Christians who refused to bow to the royal throne and worship the Caesars as gods (as was often practiced) were severely persecuted, meaning death for many disciples.

Addressing those Christians who were undergoing persecution, the writer of 1 Peter began his letter:

> Blessed be the God and Father of our Lord Jesus Christ! By his great mercy we have been born anew to a living hope through the Resurrection of Jesus Christ from the dead, and to an inheritance which is imperishable, undefiled, and unfading, kept in heaven for you, who by God's power are guarded through faith for a salvation ready to be revealed in the last time.
>
> In this rejoice, though now for a little while you may have to suffer various trials, so that the genuineness of your faith, more precious than gold which though perishable is tested by fire, may rebound to praise and glory and honor at the revelation of Jesus Christ.
>
> (1 Pet. 1:3–7)

Because we are imperfect humans in need of "refinement," like a precious metal requiring purification, we need to be purged of impurities in our faith. The writer compares this purification to the "testing" of gold, which is accomplished only by the "refiner's fire."

We can observe from this passage, however, that the opening admonition of 1 Peter was actually intended as an encouraging reminder to the persecuted to look not at the immediate pain of the fiery testing, but beyond it to the positive results the "various trials" produce:

> Having purified your souls by your obedience to the truth for a sincere love of the brethren, love one another earnestly from the heart. You have been born anew, not of perishable seed but of imperishable, through the living and abiding word of God; for
> "all flesh is like grass
> and all its glory like the
> flower of the grass.
> The grass withers, and the flower falls,
> But the word of the Lord abides for ever."
> That word is the good news which was preached to
> you.   (1 Pet. 1:22–25)

Speaking of suffering as "fire" is reflective of what we feel when we embrace pain. Fire burns and hurts! But fire also purifies and strengthens, forging toughness and durability. Just as melted gold when purified may be molded into artworks of immortal beauty or jewelry that will last and enhance the owner for years, faith that is refined through struggle with suffering is molded after the likeness of God—the one who has come into our world in the likeness of a sufferer.

From the "refiner's fire," impurities in our faith surface in our consciousness. And having recognized those impurities, we can no longer remain the same. For once we have been tempered by the discipline of dealing with painful occurrences, we can no longer be, for instance, as selfish in our relationships with others or as insensitive to their pain, as we were before. Or we may grow spiritually by learning that when it comes right down to it, we really do not trust God or anyone else. Or we may learn patience simply by *having* to practice it in searching for the roots of our struggle. In all these areas (and many more) the imperfections of our faith come to light in order that we may begin to purify ourselves of them.

Mature Faith

> *Count it all joy, my brethren, when you meet various trials, for you know that the testing of your faith produces steadfastness. And let steadfastness have its full effect that you may be perfect and complete, lacking in nothing.* (Jam. 1:2–4)

For centuries, suffering has been likened to groping in darkness, shivering out in the cold, or being stranded in a desert. Drawing from these rich resources, Martin Marty, in his wonderful book *A Cry of Absence: Reflections for the Winter of the Heart*, corresponds the changing seasons of the year to the seasons of one's spiritual life. When someone close to us dies or we experience some other kind of loss, our spirituality may have a cold wintery feeling (as opposed to a warm summery feeling when things seem to be going well). There are many persons, he says, who claim to be "spirit-filled" who never embrace or even recognize the wintery spirituality because they think it "un-Christian" to let on that things aren't going so well. "Never does the storm of a troubled heart receive its chance to be heard. The Lord satisfied every need, one hears, so it would be a sin to stare once more at the void within. Christ is the answer, the spirit is warm and no chill is ever allowed between the boards or around the windows of the soul."

As Marty suggests, it is too bad that many view denying one's suffering as the most mature and staunchly faithful way to respond to suffering in a Christian manner.

But no: Such a response is an expression of *immature* faith. It presumes that all suffering is evil and that the visitation of pain into our lives is something not to be heeded but only endured! Rather, to fail to cultivate this enormously fruitful ground for spiritual growth is to miss some of the most deeply rewarding experiences in Christian life! Although denial is a necessary coping mechanism imbedded within our souls for dealing with grief, extended denial of pain blocks spiritual and emotional growth. It is immature faith, a faith that meagerly fed and underexercised may eventually peter out altogether.

In James's epistle we read, "Count it all *joy* . . . when you meet various trials." In the previous section we read in 1 Peter, "In this *rejoice*, though now for a little while you may have to suffer various trials." Is the mature response to rejoice while we are in pain?

The words *joy* and *rejoice* as they appear in James and 1 Peter do not mean exactly what one might think at first glance. The rejoicing we find there is not a shallow, Pollyannaish refusal to admit that problems exist; rather, it is the realistic recognition of struggle bolstered by the decision to rejoice in knowing that God is working to bring one safely through the strife.

It is a very difficult achievement to be able to truly rejoice while one is suffering. Most certainly, such rejoicing will not take the form of emotional jubilance or elation. James proclaims that suffering may be counted as joy or gain when one faces the trials because the encounter with pain may produce the quality of *steadfastness*. And steadfastness, when it is allowed to bud and flower into fullness, produces the rarest of all qualities: Christian wholeness and maturity.

True Christian maturity, then, is a steadfastness that we attain not simply by enduring suffering and especially not by denying pain. It is a quality that, like any other maturity, accrues with experience, age, and a lot of willing work. It is the ability to redirect one's thoughts beyond one's own immediate woes to realize the spiritual growth that results from the tests of faith.

Therefore when suffering comes, one "rejoices." Not that one enjoys the pain; but with suffering comes a more mature faith that knows many meaningful insights and new joys await us.

Finding Meaning in Our Trials

> As he passed by, he saw a man blind from his birth.
> And his disciples asked him, "Rabbi, who sinned, this
> man or his parents, that he was born blind?" Jesus
> answered, "It was not that this man sinned, or his
> parents, but that the works of God might be made
> manifest in him. (John 9:1–3)

It was very common in biblical times as in ours, to attempt to blame physical infirmities, diseases, and personal trials on one's own sins or on the "sins of the fathers"—one's parents (see Ezekiel 18:20 and Exodus 20:5, for example). Although it is clear through modern medical diagnosis that indeed some difficulties are hereditary (such as hemophilia and cystic fibrosis) and that certain psychological disorders stem from parental "guidance" (or the lack of it), in the story retold above, Jesus makes it perfectly clear that the blind man's handicap was *not* a punishment for some long forgotten misdemeanor committed by his mother or father.

We saw earlier, in examining a passage from Hebrews, that at times we may think of our difficulties as God's way of disciplining us—teaching us as a parent teaches a child. But Jesus' words to his disciples concerning the blind man give us a clearer understanding of one kind of gain resulting from discipline: that the work of God may be displayed through growth unbounded by our inherent weakness.

Of course, in this story Jesus healed the man of his blindness, and presumably it was the healing of his blindness that manifested the work of God. Many of us who hurt desperately pray to God asking for similarly miraculous healing. Many "Christians" have made a comfortable living peddling such healing. Although much controversy surrounds the issue, many people believe they have indeed been miraculously healed of physical and mental ills. Many other *equally faithful persons* also diligently pray and still do not find themselves healed of their diseases. Do some persons happen to know a magic formula that "works" with God, while others continue to suffer only because of their ignorance? Although no one fully understands the mystery of healing, the God millions of Christians worship and serve is not a God who heals capriciously "on demand." Rather, our thinking about Divine healing needs broadening to include many differing ways in which we may receive healing and wholeness.

The *meaning* we derive from working through suffering rather than the eradication of disease from our bodies ought to be the major criterion by which we perceive "healing." Though one party in a troubled relationship might be terminally ill, the *relationship* might well be healed. Or through dealing with the hurt of infertility, a couple may find healing in accepting that infertility in no way lessens their capacity to love an adopted child. Other healing victories may result from dealing with suffering—many more ways than we have the capacity to imagine or the perception to observe.

I once conducted the funeral of a dear old friend named Grace. Only a few years before, she had experienced the loss of her husband of over fifty years. Only weeks after his burial, she learned that a malignancy was raging through her body. Through magnificent perseverance, while grieving over the loss of her husband, Grace underwent agonizing chemotherapy treatments hoping they would arrest the disease. The treatments failed to halt the spread of the disease.

Yet Grace never gave up hope that one day she would be rid of her cancer.

Her health continued to deteriorate badly, and following her long and valiant struggle, Grace died. As the one who would deliver her eulogy, I agonized over what to say about Grace's death. And I confess I was tempted by questions of why such a marvelous woman had died such a lingering and painful death. Why wasn't *she* healed? If faith and hope were the keys to unlock the door to healing, she certainly possessed them in quantity! But then I began to recall her last few months and all the many persons who came in contact with Grace: There were the many friends who stopped by or telephoned to say hello and encourage her; there was the high school youth group from our church who came Christmas caroling at her home; and there was her family, who surrounded her with their love during those last days. To all of these, Grace's words and actions were always kind and graceful. Even though she did not attempt to hide her intense pain, she also did not hide her hope that healing would come—a hope that never died, even though she did.

At the funeral, it was said of Grace, "This horrible disease may have conquered her body, but *nothing* defeated her spirit, her faith, and her hope!"

As we relate Grace's struggle to be healed with the criterion of *meaning* found in suffering (rather than in physical healing), I cannot help but feel that it was the witness of Grace's death, her clinging on to hope, that proved to be the manifestation of God's healing power! Those people who came to visit Grace as she struggled with cancer did not walk away grumbling about why God had not healed her. They left her presence *inspired* and crucially aware that in Grace they had witnessed God's display of the great power of faith and hope. What a glorious vision of the deeply meaningful ways God is with us in suffering!

Her disease was not contagious, but her hope and faith *were*. And many were healed by witnessing new meaning for themselves through her life and death.

God's power is displayed in the meaning we find in suffering and healing!

Everything Works Together

> Now hope that is seen is not hope. For who hopes for what he sees? But if we hope for what we do not see, we wait for it with patience.
> Likewise the Spirit helps us in our weakness; for we do not know how to pray as we ought, but the Spirit himself intercedes for us with sighs too deep for words. . . .
> We know that in everything God works for good with those who love him, who are called according to his purpose. *(Rom. 8:24b, 26, 28)*

If God does not necessarily punish us for misconduct, as we have learned in the story of Jesus and the blind man, God also does not necessarily reward us with good things in this life when we are good or faithful. In the Christian faith we affirm God's love and care for every person equally, no matter how good or bad we are.

Although some scriptures, especially in the Old Testament, suggest that we are rewarded for our goodness, it has long been part of the Christian theological tradition that God does not dispense rewards for good behavior as we might hand out treats to a well-behaved pet.

We know that because God cares for us like an earthly parent, God also wants the best for us. Because we know that it rains "on the just and on the unjust," while we also affirm that God naturally wants the best for us, we have a difficult time understanding how God's will operates. And when we are struggling or suffering, we may feel God's will is nowhere in evidence. Yet we read in Romans, "all things work together for good to them that love God."

Probably the best-known book concerning human understanding of God's will is Leslie Weatherhead's classic *The Will of God*. In that series of sermons, originally prepared for members of his congregation in London who were suffering the tragic consequences of World War II, Weatherhead suggested we use the words "the will of God" too loosely. We confuse ourselves by not understanding the many differing ways in which God's will is expressed and how that will works in our lives. Too often we think of God's will as being a narrow path down which we must dutifully trod. And if we choose a wrong fork in the road, we are consigned, perhaps irreparably, to the hazards of a life other than the one that God *intended* for us. Our wrong choice, we believe, is the source of all our distress.

To clarify these differing misunderstandings about God's will, Weatherhead suggested thinking of God's will in three aspects: God's *intentional* will, God's *circumstantial* will, and God's *ultimate* will.

Confusion prevails when we attribute *one aspect* of God's will to all our lives. We generally think God's will is naturally God's *intention*. But we also believe God loves us. So how can God both love us yet *intend* bad things to happen to us, especially when we try to to be good people? This confusion is apparent when a widow, for instance, speaks of her husband's death as his having been "taken" (implying, according to her perception, that God did the "taking"). Or we see confusion in another man (a faithful member of a church) who when his musically talented daughter committed suicide gained some kind of contorted comfort in telling persons attending the funeral that "God must have needed another soprano in his heavenly choir."

In Matthew 18:14 Jesus said, "It is not the will of my Father who is in heaven that one of these little ones should perish." From this scripture and many others, one may assume that it is not God's *intention* for little ones (nor, presumably, any of the rest of us) to suffer or perish. Yet we know all too well that we do. Why?

Because humans are free to serve and follow God, we are

also free to choose what is sinful or evil. And some of the sinful choices we make cause suffering for ourselves and others. Yet even within these evil or sinful *circumstances* brought about through our exercising the freedom God lovingly grants us as human beings, God still wills us to choose what is worthy (putting us on the better track toward godliness) rather than choose that which would cause further evil and suffering. So even in the worst of circumstances, when we have made the worst choices, God has a *circumstantial* will for us—one that may be a bit different from God's original intention.

Even though God allows the original *intentional* will to be thwarted (in order that we may freely choose to love and follow God) through circumstances brought about by our freedom, we above all believe that God's *ultimate* will cannot be thwarted. Of course, God's ultimate will for creation is not yet fully realized (although we believe it is realized in part). But in faith we know and hope that God's ultimate will can come to pass on earth as well as heaven. Indeed, this is our prayer when we repeat the Lord's Prayer, "Thy will be done on earth as it is in heaven."

Such an orientation helps us understand that sometimes we suffer because God loves us enough to give us the freedom to make mistakes. Without this freedom, we would be mere puppets with God pulling the strings. God loves but does not manipulate. Truly, God's perfect knowledge must "hurt God more than it hurts us." For the Almighty is certainly powerful enough to halt suffering—but because God loves us enough to give us freedom, God chooses to allow us to hurt and grow. And this is the way God has been shown to us in Christ.

The most vivid example of this principle and of Weatherhead's differentiation between God's intentional will, circumstantial will, and ultimate will may be seen in the life, death, and Resurrection of Christ. However, in Christ's life we may see that it *was not* God's initial intention that Christ come to die (we sometimes hear the prayer "Thank you, God, for sending Christ to die"), else why did Jesus travel, teach, and gather a discipleship, exhorting his hearers, "Follow me. . . ." It was God's intention that Jesus' hearers should repent, believe, and become a part of the new "kingdom," not kill him! And this kingdom, should Jesus have been followed according to God's intention, would have set in motion a revolutionary agent in our world by which the principle of love would have banished hatred, justice would have displaced inequality, and mercy would have overcome vengeance. Because of the freedom granted by God and the subsequent evil choices made by humans insensitive to God's intention—as God knew they might be—the *circumstances* arose in which Jesus was required to make a very important decision: He could either quit proclaiming the truth about God's love and human sinfulness or bear the consequences of human sinfulness by allowing himself to be killed on the cross. Although it was not God's *initial* intention that humankind reject and crucify the Messiah, the world was free to do so—and so inclined. Thus it became God's *circumstantial* will for Christ to die, in order to show the world both the depth of human sinfulness and the breadth of God's love.

The cross—the seemingly final sign of defeat for God's will in the world—became in itself an expression of God's ultimate will being accomplished. For God's *ultimate* will, a reconciliation between God and humanity, was accomplished in the outcome of the crucifixion: *Resurrection.* For in the Resurrection we see most fully God expressing the reality of hope within our world. When all seemed like death and suffering on the cross, life and hope and faith and joy exploded in the triumph of Resurrection. It is the hope of the Resurrection that allows us to endure and seek wholeness while we suffer, for now we know the crosses we bear will see us resurrected into joy and victory.

This understanding of God's will helps us realize a very important spiritual gain amid our strife. For with the apostle Paul, when we affirm that "all things work together for good," we are not saying that no circumstances arise that are not difficult or emotionally and spiritually trying. *Faith is no insurance policy against tragedy!* Yet the words of Paul come to us in our struggle, representing hope that God's ultimate will will not be denied. Through faith in God and the understanding that the divine gift of reason provides, we may have confidence that here, even in the dark night of the soul, in circumstances that seem far from the love and care God may intend, *God will help work things out*. We may not understand how. We do not need to. But with the help of hope, we may enjoy the privilege of witnessing God's wonderful power working in ways we could not possibly have anticipated.

Beginnings of Hope

> *Therefore, since we are justified by faith, we have peace with God through our Lord Jesus Christ. Through him we have obtained access to this grace in which we stand, and we rejoice in our hope of sharing the glory of God. More than that, we rejoice in our sufferings, knowing that suffering produces endurance, and endurance produces character, and character produces hope, and hope does not disappoint us, because God's love has been poured into our hearts through the Holy Spirit which has been given to us.* (Rom. 5:1–5)

Our spiritual passage from suffering through endurance to character leading to hope that "does not disappoint us" is a long perilous journey. Yet one of the greatest gains we can find in our struggle is to anchor ourselves in the reality of God's love for us. Then we have all the strength and hope we need to face whatever trials we encounter.

At the beginning of the path to hope, however, lies suffering. And it is only in the midst of suffering that we truly find endurance and character and the beginnings of hope.

The lives of countless persons stand as witness to the fact that struggle with suffering is redemptive. Although most persons engage in the struggle unwillingly, they learn through painful experience the truths taught by biblical passages we have examined.

One person whose eventual growth came about through

much suffering was a young man named Jim. Although he was bright and talented, because he always had his own way and things had generally gone well for him, he was frankly rather spoiled. His parents, like most, had wanted the best for their child; they lavished upon Jim just about everything he wanted, to the point where he expected nearly everything to be given to him.

As it came time for him to graduate from high school and decide upon college and a vocation, he decided that college was too much work and got a job working for a contracting firm. His abrupt decision bitterly disappointed his parents, who had long planned and budgeted so that he could attend a university. Some people wondered aloud whether Jim *intended* to hurt his parents.

Though Jim had made his decision, he lacked a basic direction for his life. He met a young woman and they soon became engaged to be married. But Jim became growingly disillusioned and bitter that his life as an adult seemed to consist of financial problems, work that he had found meaningless, and a future holding few prospects for improvement.

Life came crashing down on him the day he fell off an iron beam suspended more than fifty feet above the ground. Suddenly Jim found himself in a hospital with an injured spine leaving him a paraplegic. If he had been somewhat bitter before the accident, you can imagine the anger, frustration, and hopelessness he felt as he was forced into making an adjustment to such a profoundly difficult handicap.

Yet Jim was equipped with the tools he needed to fight the handicap; for despite his "attempt at hurting them," he had a supportive family, many friends who expressed their caring, and most important, he came to find he had a deep desire to struggle with his pain and realize gain.

It was not ever easy. Jim spent nearly six months in the hospital engaged in therapy that produced much pain and agonizingly slow progress. During those days of therapy, Jim had no choice but to remain in his bed, dependent on those around him. He was forced to accept that there were many things he could not do for himself. His physical powerlessness necessitated that a constant vigil be kept at his bedside. His parents and fiancée, taking turns in this service, were with him constantly, and Jim was forced to converse with them and with others who cared for him. Many friends brought cards and gifts and words of encouragement. Persons from his church also came by to offer their support and help.

Even though these many persons came by to help, Jim struggled continually with feelings of anger, bitterness, and resentment about his accident. He tried to keep his emotions bottled up inside, but there were many times he couldn't. At times he cried and rammed his fist into the pillow. He was often cross with the nurses and others who tried to help him. One day, exasperated by the constancy of the work it required to learn to cope with his paralysis, at the very edge of his endurance, Jim lashed out at a visitor from his church. Seething with resentment, he shouted, "Don't even try to talk about God to me! I don't care. Where was God when I fell? Where's God *now*!?"

The friend wasn't sure what to say, but managed to reply, "I wish I knew why you have to go through this, but I don't. But please know that God is with you and that when you fell, God was right there hurting with you! And God's with you now, helping you to get stronger."

Unlike such scenes in the movies, no fireworks went off and no climactic music accented the experience. Jim was still angry; yet this conversation was a turning point for him. He kept on working at his therapy and gradually improved. Jim never regained the use of his legs, but he learned to function proficiently in his wheelchair.

But the most strikingly miraculous part of Jim's healing process, indeed his most successful therapy, was the change in his attitude toward life. Before the accident and during therapy, Jim showed the world a sour personality that tended to repel others. But caring people stayed with him and helped him despite his bitterness. Slowly, through the process of fighting his disability, Jim began to realize that nothing in life could be taken for granted. He grew to appreciate those who cared for him rather than assume someone always would be there to provide for his needs. Even though he came to recognize the painful reality that he could never again use his legs, he also realized that he could *decide* what his attitude toward his circumstances would be. Little things suddenly meant a great deal to him. The cards, visits, and words of encouragement that Jim had scorned at first became important to him as he learned to appreciate these gestures of care and love. Jim also realized God is not far off but nearby, giving courage, comfort, and support.

Jim's story is full of pain and gain. It remains (and always will remain) painful for him that he will never again enjoy the full use of his legs. But another healing came to Jim, a deeper fulfillment in life, one he may never have known had he not experienced his tragic accident.

Jim found through his painful recovery a new assurance in himself. Not long after Jim and Jenny were married, he began his own small firm and has found his venture successful and rewarding. Although now, years later, life continues to be a struggle, Jim lives it to the fullest.

The kinds of gains to be found through dealing with pain are as many as the persons who truly embrace their pain. We must all, individually, seek out and identify those possibilities for spiritual growth toward which our pain points us. To be sure, someone is trying to teach us lessons. But it is up to us to learn!

Yet while we learn, what motivates us to continue in the always arduous, sometimes long struggle? Where can we find the strength we need to continue?

Through *hope*.

Part III: HOPE

When we become aware that we do not have to escape
our pains, but that we can mobilize them into a common
search for life, those very pains are transformed from
expressions of despair into signs of hope.

—*Henri Nouwen*

Hope and the Human Spirit

There is a crack of time, wedged between our experience of discipline and pain and the time when we feel something of the benefits of spiritual gain, when we may find it especially difficult to persist during our struggles. During this time, when we still have not attained our goals despite our having invested great amounts of energy in trying to resolve our problems, we again find ourselves confronted with difficult choices between faith and doubt, growth and decline, hope and despair. We feel we have come too far to give up, yet, are too weary from the struggle to continue.

During this troublesome phase, the cultivation of a hopeful attitude is crucial. For now, as we engage in our struggles, our temptation becomes strong to allow our attitudes to fluctuate between hope and despair. Each of us possesses a personal tolerance level for pain, and the circumstances surrounding our struggles vary. Do your own experience, background, and general outlook on life encourage a hopefulness toward the outcome of your trials? Or do you tend to approach struggle with an inward conviction that fate cannot be altered? Surrendering one's attitude toward "fate," or to a misunderstanding of God's will, may well deepen one's sense of having become a hopeless victim of circumstances perceived to be raging beyond control.

Our attitude toward hope, healing, and wholeness will greatly influence the speed and scope of the spiritual growth we derive from the discipline of dealing with pain. And the key ingredient in our approach to distress during this significant time is the mental and spiritual discipline of hope.

Many groups of people throughout history have learned the value of hope while enduring difficult, seemingly impossible times. From his study of such peoples, in particular those whose sufferings are recounted in the Old Testament, Walter Brueggemann has concluded, "Hope comes out of the public processing of pain."

From the terrifyingly gruesome and dehumanizing persecution of the European Jewish community during the insanely anti-Semitic reign of the Nazis have come many startling realizations about the human potential for evil. Yet from the valiant struggle of this people against evil; from the inexpressibly profound pain that has been processed in the years since the Holocaust—and continues to be processed by Jews and non-Jews—many positive contributions have been made to our understanding of the resiliency of the human spirit and the importance of hope.

Among the many moving personal accounts written by survivors of the Nazi death camps is Viktor Frankl's *Man's Search for Meaning.* While Frankl recounts his experiences at the personal level, he is also remarkably able, from his viewpoint as a trained, professional psychiatrist, to analyze and interpret his own feelings. He vividly details the constant threat of extinction that permeated the lives of death camp residents. They found themselves suddenly stripped of personal possessions and individual identity; and the stench from flesh-burning furnaces ever reminded them that death was as close as any minor infraction of the camp rules—or closer, according to the whims of one's captors. The Nazi death machine very efficiently pushed the experience of human suffering past any fathomable expectation of mental tolerance or physical survival.

How did some survive?

Frankl suggests that the secret not only of the prisoners' survival but also of their spiritual growth was the attitude of hope for the future.

Borrowing from the thought of Nietzsche— "He who has a *why* to live can bear with almost any *how*"—Frankl developed the understanding that even in the worst circumstances imaginable, indeed when one literally has nothing left, *no one, or nothing that happens to you, can control your own spiritual posture concerning your response to the circumstances in which you find yourself!* Frankl wrote:

> We who lived in concentration camps can remember the men who walked through the huts comforting others, giving away their last piece of bread. They may have been few in number, but they offer sufficient proof that everything can be taken from a man but one thing: to choose one's attitude in any given set of circumstances, to choose one's own way.
>
> Naturally, only a few people were capable of reaching great spiritual heights. But a few were given the chance to attain human greatness even through their apparent worldly failure and death, an accomplishment which in ordinary circumstances they would never have achieved. To the others of us, the mediocre and the half-hearted, the words of Bismarck could be applied: "Life is like being at the dentist. You always think that the worst is still to come, and yet it is already over." Varying this, we could say that most men in a concentration camp believed the real opportunities of life had passed. Yet, in reality, there was an opportunity and a challenge. One could make a victory of those experiences, turning life into an inner triumph, or one could ignore the challenge and simply vegetate.

We learn from Frankl that many of those who survived

(and many of those who did not) distinguished themselves in their suffering by accepting hopefully the challenges to growth and human dignity set before them in a world turned upside down. What made the difference was their hope—and their courage.

We cannot, must not hope to find any manner of *justification* for such suffering in terms of "valuable lessons" learned from it. Yet learn from it we must—learn, among other indelible lessons, that God has breathed into the human spirit *the ability to hope—even in the worst of circumstances*. And through hope, the human spirit is motivated to struggle mightily against agents of pain and suffering.

As we have seen, pain is a signal warning that we are in some kind of physical, emotional, or spiritual danger; struggle, with its painful discipline, is the way by which we move through the trials to healing, meaning, and wholeness. And in this crucial crack of time between embracing our pain and attaining wholeness, we can *choose* whether or not we will adopt the attitude of hope.

As persons such as Dr. Frankl show us, hope is not automatically granted to all those who struggle. But it is *available* to all those who are *willing*, through discipline, to process their pain.

Grief and Hope

*F*or several years a large number of persons in the helping professions have contributed much to our understanding of the grief process when we experience a significant loss. Most researchers and writers describe certain stages we predictably pass through in grieving. Because we have spent great amounts of time and emotional energy in nurturing relationships that are of immense value to the enrichment of our lives, when we suffer a loss we must adjust ourselves to the loss of this relationship or value by working through these stages of grief and adjustment; otherwise we may never return to "normal."

Although we do not necessarily advance through these stages in a neatly prescribed order, we can speak of a general progression of the feelings a person typically experiences while grieving. At first we feel shocked and may want to deny or avoid our feelings. We then experience the expression of our emotions, which may also manifest themselves in physical ailments or a sense of panic. We probably feel anger or guilt or a host of other emotions. Finally, usually toward the latter stages of our grief, we begin to feel hope gradually breaking through.

As we can see, hope is not the only feeling we have as we struggle toward acceptance of our loss. Most important, we note that hope does not appear early to illuminate the path we are to take on the journey to wholeness. Hope comes through *gradually*, fading in and out, struggling with all the other feelings we are having; together, those feelings will help us determine our response to the pain, separation, and loneliness we feel.

Although all the emotions we feel as we work through pain are valid, even invaluable, hope is our best friend. For it is hope that motivates us to keep on trying when we feel like quitting; it is hope that the hurt will be relieved that allows us to cry one more time even when we feel that the rivers of tears we have already shed have accomplished little; it is hope that helps us to reach out and openly share our pain with another person even when we feel we want never again to invest our trust in anyone else. It is hope that helps us work to untangle the web of twisted emotions we have tried to bury deep within our being. Hope is a struggle, but it is the struggle to free ourselves from entrapment in this web of complex and unpleasant feelings so that we may be at liberty to live a life of richly satisfying growth.

So to hope *is* to grieve and to grieve *is* to hope!

But where do we find hope?

The Road Less Traveled: God's Hope Displayed

Like all of us who struggle, suffer, learn, and grow, the human characters portrayed in many biblical stories were forced to apprehend the meaning of hope derived from painful situations in their own lives. Such stories (found in both the Old and New Testaments) that illuminate the meaning of hope are too numerous to summarize here; but we can look into several that might help us understand more fully the meaning of hope as we struggle to affirm our reality today.

That very day two of them were going to a village named Emmaus, about seven miles from Jerusalem, and talking with each other about all these things that had happened. While they were talking and discussing together, Jesus himself drew near and went with them. But their eyes were kept from recognizing him. And he said to them, "What is this conversation which you are holding with each other as you walk?" And they stood still, looking sad. Then one of them, named Cleopas, answered him, "Are you the only visitor to Jerusalem who does not know the things that have happened there in these days?" And he said to them, "What things?" And they said to him, "Concerning Jesus of Nazareth, who was a prophet mighty in deed and word before God and all the people, and how our chief priests and rulers delivered him up to be condemned to death, and crucified him. *But we had hoped that he was the one to redeem Israel.* Yes, and besides all this, it is now the third day since this happened. Moreover, some women of our company amazed us. They were at the tomb early in the morning and did not find his body; and they came back saying that they had even seen a vision of angels, who said that he was alive. Some of those who were with us went to the tomb, and found it just as the women had said; but him they did not see." And he said to them, "O foolish men, and slow of heart to believe all that the prophets have spoken! Was it not necessary that Christ should suffer these things and enter into his glory?" And beginning with Moses and all the prophets, he interpreted to them in all the scriptures the things concerning himself.

So they drew near to the village to which they were going. He appeared to be going further, but they constrained him, saying, "Stay with us, for it is toward evening and the day is now far spent." So he went in to stay with them. When he was at the table with them, he took the bread and blessed, and broke it, and gave it to them. And their eyes were opened and they recognized him; and he vanished out of their sight. They said to each other, "Did not our hearts burn within us while he talked to us on the road, while he opened to us the scriptures?" And they rose that same hour and returned to Jerusalem; and they found the eleven gathered together and those who were with them, who said, "The Lord has risen indeed, and has appeared to Simon!" Then they told what had happened on the road, and how he was known to them in the breaking of the bread.

(Luke 24:13–35 italics added)

For the disciples, too, there was that crack of time when they were tempted to give up hope. In the mere passing of a week, they had entered Jerusalem with Jesus in triumph, only to have their hopes dashed to despair in witnessing their leader's agonizing, ignominious death upon the cross. They were severely hurt and disillusioned: Jesus, the one in whom they put their hope to deliver their nation, was dead!

The two disciples walking on the road from Jerusalem to Emmaus felt hopeless. They had heard Jesus was raised from the dead, but no one had seen him. So they moped back to Emmaus, grief-stricken, bewildered, and grievously smitten in their loss of hope.

Of course, when they complained to the stranger—Jesus,

whom they failed to recognize—he told them of the *necessity* of Christ's suffering and interpreted to them "all the scriptures concerning himself." Yet it was not until Jesus entered their home and broke bread with them that they finally recognized him *and understood who he truly was and what had happened to him.*

The disciples immediately arose and journeyed a road much less traveled—the *hopeful* road from Emmaus back to Jerusalem. Unlike their travels earlier in the day on that same road coming to Emmaus, *this* trip to Jerusalem was filled with a freshly renewed hope and joy from the disciples' having seen and experienced the most hopeful sign God has ever given to our world—the resurrected Christ!

As we learned in the section "Pain and the Cross," Jesus' death was in part God's message to us that God is with us in our painful difficulties, suffering with us and for us. Similarly, the Resurrection of Jesus completes this story begun with his life and suffering death. For in beholding the entire Christ event—Jesus's life, death, and Resurrection—we see that pain and struggle are not all that we are to experience in our Christian lives. Through the Resurrection we see how God *redeems* and *reclaims* suffering and struggle and painful discipline, bringing them to a hopeful and joyous end! Of course, this does not negate the cross or its redemptive pain. Rather, through the Resurrection, God moves us *through* the pain of the cross to a newer, deeper experience of God's love.

We understand that through this pivotal event in history, God has released a mighty force into our world of struggle. The event represents hope that even in earthly life, we too will be "resurrected" from our pain and struggle, whose rigors have made us "die a bit"—"resurrected" and lifted to greater spiritual heights. The Resurrection gives us faith that even in our darkest hours, the penetrating rays of hope are never far away and will break through to illuminate our life and allow us to "run a little bit farther" down the road.

It seems we journey down the road between Emmaus and Jerusalem many times on our spiritual pilgrimage. We know it as a road of both pain and joy, both disillusionment and certainty, both despair and hope. But the longer we travel this road, the more thoroughly we are convinced that it is the same road viewed from opposite directions. In one direction we feel sorrow and pain; the other direction we may travel is hope.

The story of Christ's Resurrection teaches us that in the midst of our struggle, we have the option of taking the "road less traveled"—the road from Emmaus back to Jerusalem; the journey of hope. And on that road, we find that our pain and despair are redeemed.

The Hope of God's People

*T*here is a sense in which we are always in that crack of time when we travel the Emmaus-Jerusalem road, with its ever-lurking temptation toward hopelessness. Other biblical stories convey this truth to us because we recognize that they are mirrors of our own frustrations and struggles. We have seen in the "lament" Psalms the despairing cry of the psalmist who wonders where God has gone and even questions God's wisdom in allowing such pain and suffering to exist in the world. Yet just as we see the message of pain, gain, and hope revealed in the words of the New Testament writings, we see hope portrayed also in the Psalms and in the history of God's people, the Israelites. Their story, told in the Old Testament, relates not only their questioning of God, it displays also the great trust they felt that in the end God would act to deliver Israel (as well as the individual sufferer) from pain and distress and grant her new life.

This passage from despair to hope often takes place within a particular Psalm. For example in chapter 1 we read from Psalm 13:

> How long, O Lord? Wilt thou
> forget me for ever?

How long wilt thou hide thy
 face from me?
How long must I bear pain in my soul,
 and have sorrow in my heart all the day?

(Ps. 13:1–2)

But the Psalm continues in hope:

But I have trusted in thy steadfast love;
 my heart shall rejoice in thy salvation.
I will sing to the Lord,
 because he has dealt bountifully with me.

(Ps. 13:5–6)

We also looked at the 38 Psalm:

My wounds grow foul and fester
 because of my foolishness,
I am utterly bowed down prostrate;
 all the day I go about mourning.

I am utterly spent and crushed;
 I groan because of the tumult of my heart.

(Ps. 38:5–6, 8)

But the Psalm continues in hope:

But for thee, O Lord, do I wait;
 it is thou, O Lord my God, who wilt answer.

For I am ready to fall,
 and my pain is ever with me.

Do not forsake me, O Lord!
 O my God, be not far from me!
Make haste to help me,
 O Lord, my salvation.

(Ps. 38:15, 17, 21–22)

And Psalm 42:

> I say to God, my rock:
>   "Why hast thou forgotten me?
> Why go I mourning because of the oppression of
>   the enemy?"
> As with a deadly wound in my body,
>   my adversaries taunt me,
> while they say to me continually,
> "Where is your God?"

(Ps. 42:9–10)

But the Psalm continues in hope:

> Why are you cast down, O my soul,
>   and why are you disquieted within me?
> *Hope in God*; for I shall again praise him,
>   my help and my God.

(Ps. 42:11 italics added)

Revealed in these scriptures is a dual recognition of pain and distress, along with a strong expression of resolve to place hope in God.

The roots of hope run deep in ancient Israel's history. And the very basis for the hope of God's people is placed in one pivotal event: the Exodus of the Israelites from Egypt into the Promised Land. A very short time passed between Jesus' Crucifixion and his Resurrection; but the ancient pilgrims wandered in the wilderness longing and hoping for the Promised Land for forty years! Before undertaking this miserably long journey, God's people spent many years as slaves in Egypt, crying out for God to hear them. Many who started the journey never saw its completion.

All generations of Jewish people since then have remembered and celebrated God's deliverance of their ancestors (and thereby themselves as well) from bondage in Egypt. The remembrance of this historical event has provided the primary basis for belief in hope that pervades Jewish thought—and

49

provides invaluable help to Christian thought as well. For not only can Jewish people remember and celebrate the deliverance of their forefathers and foremothers; through this remembrance they also celebrate *their own* present deliverance from bondage, pain, and oppression. Time after time the biblical witness recalls this focal event in history as if it were being relived in the present (see Ps. 80:8, Judg. 6:7–9, 1 Sam. 10:17–18, Josh. 24:16–17). This continual process of dealing with pain and celebrating deliverance has produced a history of hope unequaled in our world.

The basic hope that God would deliver God's people allowed the prophet Jeremiah to proclaim to those persons who were suffering the separation and pain of exile in a foreign land:

> I will fulfill to you my promise and bring you back to this place. For I know the plans I have for you, says the Lord, plans for *shalom* and not for evil, to give you a future and a hope.... You will seek me and find me; when you seek me with all your heart, I will be found by you, says the Lord, and I will restore your fortunes.... (Jer. 29:10–14)
> (Translation from *Living Toward a Vision*, Walter Brueggemann, New York: United Church Press, 1982.)

That vision of peace (*shalom*) includes love, hope, faith, fulfillment, justice, mercy, and many more qualities. But those who suffer find in it what sufferers have found there for many centuries: a vision of hope and meaning in life. We are God's people, and despite evidence to the contrary, God has *not* forgotten us, and will remain faithful.

Yet quite disconcertingly, Jeremiah also notes:

> But seek the *shalom* of the city where I have sent you into exile, and pray to the Lord on its behalf, for in its *shalom* you will find your *shalom*. (Jer. 29:7)
> (Tr. from *Living Toward a Vision*)

This ancient truth startles those of us who wrestle with the spiritual struggles of our own personal "exile" or "bondage." For in Jeremiah, and ultimately in our own life, we learn that it is in the very midst of the exile that we learn the lessons God teaches about wholeness and wellness (*shalom*). In this struggle, which we by no means enjoy, we also, surprisingly, find an unexpected gift: peace, meaning, and spiritual well-being—*shalom*.

We can see that the hope God gave to the people of Israel was the same hope that He displayed in Christ: God is present in the world, actively working through our suffering to offer hope and healing. But as we have seen, it is not hope for deliverance from suffering but hope in deliverance *through* pain and discipline.

Endless Hope?

Jesus' words from Psalm 22, uttered on the cross, "My God, my God, why hast thou forsaken me?" also end in hope affirmed by his Resurrection.

Here is some of the remainder of Psalm 22:

> But thou, O Lord, be not far off!
> O thou my help, hasten to my aid!
>
> From thee comes my praise in the great
> congregation,
> my vows I will pay before those who fear him.
> The afflicted shall eat and be satisfied;
> those who seek him shall praise the Lord!
> May your hearts live for ever!
>
> All the ends of the earth shall remember and turn
> to the Lord;

And all the families of the nations shall worship
    before him.
For dominion belongs to the Lord,
    and he rules over the nations.

Yea, to him shall all the proud of the earth bow
    down;
    before him shall bow all who go down to the
    dust,
    and he who cannot keep himself alive.

Posterity shall serve him;
    men shall tell of the Lord
    to the coming generation,
and proclaim his deliverance to a people yet
    unborn,
that he has wrought it.

(Ps. 22:19, 25–31)

When it may have seemed like Jesus was speaking of a
hopeless end to his life, we see from the Psalm quoted that
he was also proclaiming an endless hope. It is a hope to be
passed from one generation to the next with its one basic
message: God delivers God's people! And through this process
of deliverance, God's people grow in spirit.

Indeed, this hope has been passed to us today through
many generations, and we see it well in the lives of many
persons around us. We earlier saw hope in the life of Jim in
his struggle with his accident as we also saw hope in Grace's
life as she fought a terminal disease.

And you remember William Sloane Coffin's sermon
delivered shortly after the death of his son, Alex.

Coffin concluded his sermon that day,

And of course I know, even when pain is deep,
that God is good. "My God, my God, why hast thou
forsaken me?" Yes, but at least, "My God, my God";
and the psalm only begins that way, it doesn't end

that way. As the grief that once seemed unbearable begins to turn now to bearable sorrow, the truths of the right biblical passages are beginning, once again, to take hold: "Cast thy burden upon the Lord and He shall strengthen thee"; "Weeping may endure for a night, but joy cometh in the morning"; "Lord, by that favor thou has made my mountain to stand strong"; "for thou has delivered my soul from death, mine eyes from tears, and my feet from falling." "In this world ye have tribulation, but be of good cheer, I have overcome the world." "The light shines in darkness, and the darkness has not overcome it."

And finally I know that when Alex beat me to the grave, the finish line was not Boston Harbor in the middle of the night. If a week ago Monday a lamp went out, it was because, for him at least, the Dawn had come.

So I shall—so let us all—seek consolation in that love which never dies, and find peace in the dazzling grace that always is.

Our *hope* as we face the difficulties of life is in the never-ending love God has shown our world.

Part IV: HELP

We do not exist for ourselves (as the center of the universe), and it is only when we are fully convinced of this fact that we begin to love ourselves properly and thus also love others. What do I mean by loving ourselves properly? I mean, first of all, desiring to live, accepting life as a very great gift and a great good, not because of what it gives us, but because of what it enables us to give others.

—*Thomas Merton*

Helpful Prayer

In this process of spiritual growth and learning, a higher stage in our development comes in recognizing the infinite number of ways God offers help in our distress. Among these channels through which we receive God's help, the most direct dimension of assistance comes through prayer.

We acknowledged in the first chapter that we sometimes feel "alone with pain," since no one else can suffer or grow for us. And here's another truth: No matter how alone we may feel, we are never truly alone in our suffering. For when we feel alone and long for help from the Source of all growth and hope, God's presence fulfills our yearning through the discipline of prayer.

However, the kind of help many of us seek through prayer is burdened with misunderstandings. Too often prayer is likened to the presentation of our own personal shopping list to a celestial Santa Claus who promptly delivers the goodies in neatly wrapped packages. And if the packages don't arrive exactly as we asked, and right on our schedule, we nag more diligently until we either get what we wanted or give up! Obviously, this is not true prayer.

Although petitioning God for our needs is certainly part of healthy prayer, true communication with God is infinitely more meaningful and powerful. When we learn and begin to yield to prayer as communication *from* God rather than as a shopping spree, we instantaneously open ourselves to profoundly satisfying and healing experiences of God's help.

To write or read about the elusive experience of God through prayer is an incredibly imprecise task. For in speaking of something so mysterious and personal, words become clumsy almost spurious tools in communicating the meaning of a deep relationship and consciousness of God. Even so it might be helpful to attempt an outline of some general guidelines for prayer.

The long and rich history of literature about the experience of prayer has in recent years exploded with renewed interest. Among the many aspects of prayer that have received much discussion have been the disciplines of silence and solitude, meditation and contemplation, and translating prayer into relationships with others.

In our earlier discussion we stressed discipline, not as a form of punishment but as an opportunity for growth. Just as athletes must "work out" regularly, we must view prayer as the "gymnasium of the soul." But in this arena, most of us feel like weaklings. When it comes to prayer, we assume that we lack the understanding and stamina required to be effective.

The discipline of prayer should not be viewed as a slavish duty to which one must expend every ounce of strength trying to reach an unattainable goal. Rather prayer should be thought of as a liberating discipline that opens doors to greater celebration through receiving God's healing and sustaining presence. Of course, like any other discipline it is difficult (and painful) to grow in prayer. And there is only one way to learn: Pray!

It seems we humans have an inclination to refuse the medicine that can heal us. And because we avoid discipline, we find that, as Douglas Steere wrote, our "greatest pain comes from the tightness of our grip on that which holds us back."

For this reason, while in the midst of our struggle, we

may find it hard to engage the discipline of prayer. In *The Workbook on Intercessory Prayer*, Maxie Dunnam tells of having the same problem. It seems that as he was praying for a retreat he was to lead, excruciating pain throbbed in his shoulders and neck. Because of this discomfort he was not sleeping and having difficulty praying—and release from his pain was part of what he was praying for! Then he said God's word to him was, "until you are relieved of your pain, use it as a call to prayer."

Because our discomfort might be a hindrance to learning the discipline of prayer, I believe this insight of using pain as a "call to prayer" is an excellent one for us to remember. Yet another important element of Dunnam's experience was that his learning did not proceed from what he *told* God but from the word of God to him. It is only in the context of silence and solitude, however, that such insight can come.

To put the problem simply: Most of us are too busy blabbing at God in prayer to ever be able to listen to what God might be "saying" to us. Of course, God doesn't shout audibly in our ears—but most certainly God "speaks" to us, usually in a "whisper." With our verbose prayers, frantic pace of activity, and constant blasting of music in our ears through inventions such as the Walkman, there is little way short of battery failure that we can hear God "whisper."

But making the effort to sustain disciplined silence and solitude with God grants us enormous possibilities for spiritual growth. For in regular aloneness and silence we can more ably discern the "still small voice" whispering in our spiritual ear. Here is where we learn pain's lessons.

This process of communicating and learning in prayer has been called meditation or contemplation. In our first attempts at this type of prayer, (which might be unfamiliar to many of us), we may become discouraged because we find that our minds wander. We start out to pray, but we find ourselves thinking about all sorts of other things—daydreaming! Or we may suddenly realize we are replaying recent conversations or remembering past experiences we either wanted to recall or were trying to forget.

Rather than castigate ourselves for a lack of discipline in retaining "spiritual" thoughts, why not view these images as part of our prayer? From these random thoughts and images may come significant insights and feelings about ourselves and our relationship with God. In this meditation, we may recall and contemplate meaningful scriptures or other readings that have help to offer in our present circumstances. Advice from friends or family members may be placed in our thoughts, giving us encouragement and hope. We may even drift into sleep as a gift of renewal amidst our hard work! The fresh images and energizing insights found in these times are virtually limitless!

In these "depths" of communication with God, you will find that words grow increasingly less important as a tool of communication. Sobs and tears, a grunt of frustration, or a sigh of pain or relief may all be considered nonverbal yet extremely communicative prayer. The apostle Paul expressed this in the following verses:

> Likewise, the Spirit helps us in our weakness; for we do not know how to pray as we ought, but the Spirit himself intercedes for us *with sighs too deep for words.* And he who searches the hearts of men knows what is the mind of the Spirit, because the Spirit intercedes for the saints according to the will of God.
>
> (Rom. 8:26–27 italics added)

Then he reminds us that "we know that in everything God works for good..." (Rom. 8:28).

When "sighs" replace words and communion with God is impressed on us through silence and solitude, meditation and contemplation, one might assume this achievement to equal a constant state of bliss wherein the world's cares are blocked out and can no longer harm us. Paradoxically, this type of prayer leads us not toward strange detachment from the world but a more vital engagement in it. As Henri Nouwen has written, "We are speaking here about a mystery for which words are inadequate. It is the mystery that the heart, which is the center of our being, is transformed by God into his own heart, a heart large enough to embrace the entire universe. Through prayer we can carry in our heart all human pain and sorrow, all conflicts and agonies, all torture and war, all hunger, loneliness, and misery, not because of some great psychological or emotional capacity, but because God's heart has become one with ours."

In reaching inwardly through prayer, we mysteriously find ourselves reaching out to others both to receive their help and to offer help to them.

Helpful People

No one can successfully cope with life's pain and struggle, nor its joys and successes without help from other people and God. Yet many among us apparently believe that living was meant to be a painless activity. Modern-day culture (especially American culture) does its best to brainwash us into believing in the sufficiency—indeed, the moral superiority—of self-reliance. Permeating our thinking is the image of the self-made man who by hard work and, supposedly, no help from anyone else made his way to the top of the ladder and attained well-deserved respect, wealth, and independence. Such a myth is based on, and fosters, the illusion that "strong" people do not need anyone else. But even in our more modestly "inde-pendent" acts, we all depend on others, often unseen others. Going to the grocery store to choose and buy our food—or finding ourselves so "independent" that we can rely on a dietician to plan our meals, a shopper to fetch the ingredients, and a chef to prepare them for us—do we pause to consider how many people are involved in the process of making our food available? At the least, farmers, fertilizer dealers, farm implement makers, butchers, food processors, and grocery personnel are involved in this process before most of us see the finished products. How silly for us to think by simply earning a living that we "made it" without any help or that we do not need help from other people. We are not totally independent; we are dependent in millions of ways we take for granted daily.

Yet this "independence" illusion creeps into our religious thinking as well. We may acknowledge the help of God when we "make it" (how many times do you hear athletes thank God for their victories yet strangely not for their defeats); but we rarely give other people the opportunity to help us, because we think we don't, or in any case shouldn't, need any help outside our religion.

We all need to have a strong basic belief—before God and ourselves—in our worth as individuals. In fact, much of Christian theology is based on God's having placed infinite worth on each human being. That belief demands that we value ourselves. But a belief that just "me and Jesus" can face the world of "fleshly evil" is misbegotten, even though it is propounded by popular preachers of the "electronic church." It closes off countless possibilities for receiving the help God offers through other people! When one allows oneself to realize he or she is not completely independent and does not need to be—when we realize we do need other people to love us, appreciate us, and help us—we then begin to take giant leaps in the spiritual growth we experience in the context of community. We no longer fear we may explode from having bottled up our emotions, as well we might in continuing to face pain and the challenges of hope, all by ourselves.

Through sharing, we find out we are not at all "weird" for feeling such strong emotions, as we may have thought we were because no one else *seemed* to feel the way we did. Through sharing our pain with others, whether individually or in groups, we find the greatest source of hope and comfort imaginable. And from the comfort we enjoy from others' care, we experience more significant growth and healing. Such contact also gives us the perfect opportunity to discover others who are experiencing similar difficulties so that we may offer our help to them!

Help and Healing

A young couple I know very well decided to take one of their frequent evening drives in the country in the twilight of a gloriously colorful summer sunset. Only a few months before, the two had moved into a new community. They often took these country drives to get away from the frustrations and struggles of their new situation.

Things had not gone well since they had relocated. In the community from which they came, they had enjoyed many friends, the security and satisfaction of meaningful careers, an active and friendly church, the familiarity of the home they enthusiastically decorated together, and many other comforts, relationships, and benefits from having lived in this community for several years.

Yet they decided to relocate to this new community because one of them was offered a promotion and a raise in salary. Things were not as cozy or comfortable in their new city, they quickly learned. Many things they had taken for granted in their former community, things like knowing how to get to the grocery store, choosing and making appointments with doctors and dentists, getting to a bank—all these simple activities became a frustrating ordeal involving searching tiny unfamiliar maps for tiny unfamiliar streets. Everywhere they went there were strangers where before there had been friends. They found themselves incredibly lonely and very much hurt that no one knew them well enough to care or help.

In addition, the young woman's job for which they had moved turned out to be quite different from what they had expected (and by no means a positive experience). Besides all these things, the husband had resigned a fulfilling job only to find long waiting lists of job seekers ahead of him.

At times the couple's country drives were crying sessions during which they would release their feelings of loneliness, hurt, anger, and frustration. Vaguely, they hoped things would get better. Yet they couldn't understand what had happened: They had planned so well. They had gone to church and prayed about whether to accept the move. They had tried to be nice to people they encountered in their new environment; but no one, it seemed, was nice back. "Where is God?" they wondered.

As they were driving on one particularly magnificent evening, suddenly the car quit working. Stranded deep in the country, they tried to repair the car but to no avail. What else could go wrong!

Just as they were ready to begin the long walk back to town, an elderly man in a rusted truck pulled up and said, "Can I give you some help?"

"No, thanks," the young man answered, "it would be too much trouble."

With a sly smile and a chuckle, the man responded, "If it were too much trouble, I wouldn't have offered. Climb in!"

The couple reluctantly joined him, and as they were returning toward town, the man told them, "You know, I usually don't go home that way where your car was. But I just thought I would tonight."

"We're glad you did. We appreciate your help," the woman of the couple haltingly answered (since it was clear her husband was still too angry about the car to make conversation).

"Well, I'm glad when people let me help 'em. They don't all do, you know," the old man said as an aside. "Yes, ever since my wife died and people did things that showed me how much they cared—bringing over food, sending sympathy cards, stuff like that—ever since then, I decided to help somebody out whenever I could. It was people helping me through a hard time that made the difference. It's funny. I miss my wife more than anything. But in a way, I'm thankful that I finally learned how much people can care. I don't think I really knew that before."

As the man let the couple off at their home, he said, "God bless you, now!"

"God just did."

Feeling quite differently now than when they had left the

house, even with their car still stranded out in the countryside, the couple mysteriously felt made anew with hope from their encounter with the old man. It seemed as if God had visited them to say, "I am with you. I am helping you. Things will get better."

What do you suppose they would have felt like if they had walked home?

One might say this meeting was coincidence; certainly it was a meeting by chance. Does that make it any less an encouraging reminder of "no pain, no gain"?

The encounter was, I believe, the work of God's people helping one another by offering hope and support in the midst of struggle. For when we feel like we are alone and stranded in a strange, even hostile, territory, *there are plenty of God's people around who will help if we allow them to.* But allowing them to help means admitting to ourselves that we cannot solve all our problems by ourselves. We need help!

The young couple began to realize that they needed help; they couldn't face all their problems alone. Realizing that their past attitude toward new acquaintances was a friendliness more passive than active, they invited people over to their home in an effort to make new friends. They selected a church with many activities to share faith through personal contact with others. They searched for ways in which they might be of service to their new neighbors and learned that many persons in the neighborhood were also searching for friendly people with whom to associate. Most important, the couple eventually came to realize that their pain and loneliness were ways through which they perceived their needs and began to seek help. This whole process was set in motion because they reluctantly accepted help from a man who knew what it felt like to be stranded on a lonely road!

God supplies help in many more ways than we can possibly imagine or perceive. But when we learn to be sensitive to the avenues of help God offers, we open ourselves to receiving previously blocked inspiration of hope, faith, and love. For if our hurt is isolation, God comes as a welcomed friend to help share our burden. If our pain is grief over the loss of a beloved, God helps ease our hurt through the many expressions of care and concern people so marvelously give when they see a person in need. If our struggles are related to the many stresses placed on our marriage and family relationships, God's help may come through seeking and receiving the benefit of professional counseling or by bending the ear of good, caring, listening friends.

Pain is our friend when its discomfort motivates us to seek help, and not keep our difficulties to ourselves.

When pain is held inside, it intensifies and eats away at our soul like acid; but when it is openly shared, it can be wondrously lessened. Of course, sharing pain and problems is not easy. It takes a willingness to reveal, to ourselves and others, our vulnerability—and that takes courage. Just as athletes repeat the phrase "no pain, no gain," they also sometimes say, "*no guts, no glory.*" Courage is not as difficult to come by when a person with whom you choose to share your pain is someone in whom you know you can confidently place your trust. Although choosing your confidants involves risk that should not be taken lightly, you may know many trustworthy persons who would be very willing to offer their help. But they cannot read your mind; you must have the courage to come forward. Your action will not only benefit you, it will benefit them, too! For most of the time we find we are never happier than when we are doing something to help someone else. And in this helpful process we all find healing.

The Wounded Healer

Probably the most significant spiritual gain we can reap from our struggles is to learn that help must flow from God through us to others, even while we feel hurt ourselves. For showing others we care is the very core of what it means to practice Christian love as it has been demonstrated to us through Jesus Christ.

One of the most spiritually sensitive persons in our world today is Henri Nouwen. Among his many insightfully written books is *The Wounded Healer*. In describing the particular difficulties of ministry in our complex contemporary world, Nouwen notes that many people in modern society suffer because they are "wounded" by a general lack of hope, by loneliness, and by an increasing "rootlessness" experienced widely within our culture. Nouwen suggests that one is a successful and effective minister to others only to the degree that one is open to experiencing personally these "wounds" of society; that only by truly feeling the hurt of the world can one understand how to help the wounded.

Nouwen's idea of the "wounded healer" is not only extremely helpful among professional clergy in their efforts to help others, it is of immense value to *all* who hurt from the painful wounds of modern struggles. For the most important feature of the wounded healer image is that it turns our primary attention away from our own hurtful wounds toward becoming a helpful "healer" of the wounds of those around us! Becoming a wounded healer carries with it tremendous responsibility: We can no longer deny or ignore our own pain, for this denial robs us of our vital ability to empathize with our brothers and sisters who also hurt. In refusing to suffer our hurts alone, we learn that many other wounded healers stand with us.

Living as a wounded healer not only increases our responsibility, it also mysteriously lessens our load.

So becoming a wounded healer, paradoxically, is a means through which we receive God's helpful healing for our own wounds, by reaching out to help God heal others. Until we break out of a preoccupation with our own pain by reaching out *from* our pain to help others, we will not fully experience the richest dimensions and meaning of spiritual growth and healing. All pain, gain, hope, help, joy, and true fulfillment are felt only within the context of our relationships with other people—community. And our community is found only in that degree to which we are willing to move beyond ourselves to consider the needs of others. Our community may be found partly in a church group, but all of us have innumerable other opportunities to share with others. The important fact is that our pain must *find* its help and *give* its help within a group of people for our spiritual growth to have its deepest meaning.

Of course, this doesn't mean blurting out every little discomfort every time you go to church or bravely "martyring" yourself by condescendingly stooping to help others. Surprisingly many persons make a career out of such "sharing" (which is really complaining and pointless egoism). We all learn to avoid asking some people how they are feeling for fear they will indeed tell us ("terrible"), just as we don't ask others because they seem unable to be honest ("everything is going great"). True wounded healers learn when it is appropriate to share and when it is most helpful to allow another the chance to receive care. When we are consistently faithful in temporarily withholding expression of our own needs in order that others may reveal theirs, we will always find that the right time will come for us to share our burdens as well.

Being a wounded healer is not a difficult process to understand—yet it is the most difficult task we will ever attempt. It may be as simple as nodding your head in affirmation of a friend's intimate sharing of his burden or as difficult as facing a long-lingering death of a much-loved family member or friend. Yet it is this paradoxical relationship between wounds and healing, life and death, pain and gain, hope and help, guts and glory, and all the rest—*it is only in allowing ourselves to feel the intensity of these seemingly opposite emotions that we find ourselves living at the very core of the life God graciously gives us!* Here the depths of life's spiritual meaning soak into our being. May our goal be to stand ever in joyous awe of the splendor of the gift of living! Here, at the core, pain and gain merge in such a way that it no longer matters so much *why* we suffer, for our attention is too intensely focused on probing the meaning of God's creation to be distracted with pain and discipline.

I must admit I have known few people who have attained such spiritual heights. I admire them as one admires the lofty achievements of a mountain climber from the safe, level plains below. Yet I will never cease to be awestruck at the knowledge that those who have scaled the highest spiritual peaks are also among those who have suffered the most pain. These persons, it seems, are like Moses, who led his people from bondage and struggled up the mountain to stand in the very presence of God. By his experience, Moses was transformed; he had lived for a moment or two in divine splendor.

One such person I have had the privilege to know was Mance Gilliam, who lived in Durham, North Carolina.

Mance

Mance was the youngest of twelve brothers and sisters born into a Southern black sharecropper's family during the earliest part of this century. It was his mother's dream that one of her children attend college.

Now, one can only imagine some of the special difficulties and struggles involved in sending a young black man, however intelligent, through college in the racial climate of the 1920s South. But although there was little money among the Gilliams, the whole family cooperated in pooling available financial resources, funneling cash downward so that the youngest member might receive the education that had long been Mance's mother's dream. Through his family's love and labors (and much hard work of his own), Mance successfully graduated and began work for the North Carolina Mutual Insurance Company, then one of the largest black-owned businesses in the nation, and advanced to the position of vice-president supervising all the company's field agents. Mance's career was highly successful and rewarding.

But he did not reserve his skills and talents for business use only. Mance was also a leader in his local church as well as within the wider world of his denomination, the African Methodist Episcopal Church, Zion. He was elected a delegate to every national general conference between 1948 and 1976. Through his extensive travels and influence in the black community throughout the South, Mance attained a position from which he assisted eight financially struggling black colleges in remaining open during the Depression years. His work with these institutions of higher learning, one of which he felt privileged to have attended, was his proudest achievement.

When I first met Mance, he had been "retired" for over ten years and had aged to his late seventies. He was working as a volunteer fund-raiser for a senior citizens agency serving mostly lower-income urban dwellers. With a spry spring in his step and an unmistakable vibrancy in his smile, he greeted each of the senior citizens every day as he came into work at the senior center. Mance volunteered an average of thirty to forty hours per week to the agency. No one who witnessed his energy and attitude could have found it easy to believe he was older than many of the residents!

In long talks together over lunch, Mance shared with me wonderful stories about many of the struggles of his life. He filled me with inspiration by communicating not just the fascinating events, but also his own profoundly perceptive spiritual interpretation of each experience. In all his struggles with racist whites seeking to bankrupt the financially fragile small Southern black colleges, Mance saw a larger spiritual battle being waged between prejudice and divine justice. In his work for the insurance company he had seen God's care for a painfully oppressed people at work, providing valuable financial protection to those who could find such security nowhere else. And in his work with the senior citizens agency, Mance saw the opportunity to serve those who had not been as fortunate as he, devoting long hours and much energy to help them out. For Mance, such efforts were not woeful duty; they were spontaneous acts of gratitude to the people he felt had helped him all his life.

In all these many activities taking place over a significant period of time, Mance had seen and faced more painful conflict than I had even imagined. And for him each event was a spiritual struggle. To Mance there was no separation between the sacred and the secular. His career, church work, and volunteerism were all one and the same: they were service to God and they were a struggle. It was his ability to face—even seek out—such painful experience in this spirit that made Mance one of the most remarkable persons I have ever known.

As a young and inexperienced student preparing for the ministry, one day I complained to Mance about some of the particular sacrifices the church expects professional ministers to make. Mance lightheartedly chuckled—and gave me some advice I would remember.

"Even though I wasn't a preacher, I once wrestled with that devil, too," he began. "One time, I remember, there was a Sunday morning when I was thinking hard about dumping the whole thing. I was tired of fighting all that mess out there," he said with a sweeping gesture seeming to suggest he was talking about the whole world of strife. "I was working with those colleges in Birmingham and Atlanta that were having a hard time and were calling on me. Oh, it was a mess. Everybody fussing and carrying on, wringing their hands over what we were going to do. I felt like I could take no more, and I'll tell you I was wrestling with the temptation to give up the fight."

Then Mance leaned over the table and opened his eyes wide and said, "But I went to church that Sunday morning anyway. And do you know what the preacher talked about? He talked about Saint Paul telling Titus to stay in Crete. You know that story how in Paul's letter to young Titus he told him to stay in Crete and preach the Word. Now Titus didn't *want* to stay there. Crete was an awful place—full of false preachers and everybody wrangling amongst themselves. But Paul said to Titus,"—Mance spoke slowly, in a whisper, as he pointed and leaned even closer—"Stay in Crete, Titus. Stay in Crete."

Then Mance sat back, suddenly relaxed, and said, "He was talking right to me, you see. It was like God was saying to me in that mess I was in, 'Mance, stay in Crete; stay in Birmingham.' When I heard those words that day, I just couldn't give up. We kept on fighting, and before long we had convinced those old Bull Conner boys in Birmingham to help us keep that school open."

But then Mance's fierce intensity returned as he again pointed and leaned forward toward me. "Son, what I'm saying to you is stay in Crete. Stay in Crete. I know it's a mess and a struggle. But stay in Crete!"

I will never forget the way he looked at me as he said those words. I once heard someone say, "If you haven't seen God in the eyes of another human being, you haven't seen God!" That day one could not help but see God in the eyes of Mance. And hearing those words "Stay in Crete!" had much the same effect on me as "No pain, no gain!" directed toward me much later by my jogging partner. In both cases those were words of help from God, encouraging me in my spiritual struggle to continue on a little further so that I might learn and grow.

Less than two weeks after delivering his inspiring speech to me, Mance was hospitalized. After only a few more days, he died. I learned that for several years Mance had known he was terminally ill with cancer. He had chosen to tell this news only to his closest friends and a very few church members, because he wanted to keep on working and helping people.

Months later while recalling his "stay in Crete" admonition, I thought of how Mance himself lived its essence to the very end. Even while bearing the deep wounds and battle scars left from a life full of strife (and while others might have thought he could simply "throw in the towel," already having done more than his part), in an astounding display of spiritual maturity, he spent his last days helping to heal the hurts of others. He was working for the comfort of others even in his own great discomfort.

Such lofty heights of spiritual growth not many of us can scale. Yet the spiritual truth of Mance Gilliam's experience applies to us all: Through his pain from working to relieve the difficulties and suffering of others, Mance embraced the burden and the joy of finding that pain and gain do journey together in life. Surely he inspired many others to emulate his healing example.

The philosopher and psychologist William James once said, "The greatest use of a life is to spend it on something that outlasts it." Mance Gilliam demonstrated to me that nothing outlasts the influence of spiritual growth learned through struggle, discipline, and pain.

POSTSCRIPT

> *The world breaks everyone and afterward many are
> strong at the broken places.*
>
> —*Ernest Hemingway*

*A*fter looking more closely at pain and gain, we still cannot
explain the "curious paradox." Even more troublesome is the
fact that our world contains millions of people keenly aware
that they experience *much* pain and *no* gain. The agonizing
words of Jesus—"Why?"—will continue to echo in the hearts
not only of all who must struggle with personal pain but also
for those who must witness the tremendous amount of inno-
cent and senseless suffering all too easily found around the
globe.

So the path of spiritual growth turns us ultimately toward
a more global perspective on our problems. For in the midst
of the trials we experience personally, it may be helpful to
ponder the old Byzantine proverb recalled by Don Paarlberg,
former assistant secretary of agriculture and a specialist in
world hunger, in his book *Farmers of Five Continents*:

> He who has bread has many problems.
> He who lacks bread has only one problem.

If our own pain and discipline remind us of our personal dependence upon God, the large-scale suffering from the "one problem" we witness in our world challenges us to deepen our commitment toward alleviating life's most crucial problems. Indeed, the same principles of pain and growth are applicable to the problems facing our nations: we must grapple with these difficulties and grow toward meaningful solutions if we are to survive. It is and will continue to be a struggle.

Yet we learn, as M. Scott Peck put it, "Life is difficult." And "Once we truly know that life is difficult—once we truly understand and accept it—then life is no longer difficult. Because once it is accepted, the fact that life is difficult no longer matters." When we accept that pain and discipline are an integral part of spiritual growth, personally and globally, we then learn to focus on continuing growth not present hurts.

This gives us hope to keep trying and dreaming. It is dreaming of this hopeful day that Mary Ann Bernard has expressed in her poem "Resurrection."

Long, long, long ago;
Way before this winter's snow
First fell upon these weathered fields;
I used to sit and watch and feel
And dream of how the spring would be,
When through the winter's stormy sea
She'd raise her green and growing head,
Her warmth would resurrect the dead.

Long before this winter's snow
I dreamt of this day's sunny glow
And thought somehow my pain would pass
With winter's pain, and peace like grass
Would simply grow. The pain's not gone.
It's still as cold and hard and long
As lonely pain has ever been,
It cuts so deep and far within.

Long before this winter's snow
I ran from pain, looked high and low
For some fast way to get around
Its hurt and cold. I'd have found,
If I had looked at what was there,
That things don't follow fast or fair.
That life goes on, and times do change,
And grass does grow despite life's pains.

Long before this winter's snow
I thought that this day's sunny glow,
The smiling children and growing things
And flowers bright were brought by spring.
Now, I know the sun does shine,
That children smile, and from the dark, cold, grime
A flower comes. It groans, yet sings,
And through its pain, its peace begins.

Mary Ann Bernard

ABOUT THE AUTHOR

John Wimmer is a United Methodist Minister who has served churches in North Carolina and Indiana. He is a graduate and Merit Scholar of Duke University Divinity School and is currently pursuing his doctorate in American Church History at the University of Chicago Divinity School.

No Pain, No Gain is Mr. Wimmer's first book.